tmare
gland
An A–Z

Kotaro Sarai is a twenty-five-year-old businessman. He came to England in September 1994 to study the language and learn the ways of Western people. He failed comprehensively.

The following pages record his thoughts, feelings and fantasies during his stay in England.

Colin Lynes English tutor to Kotaro Sarai (apparently)

Colin Lynes cropped up in my life in September 1994 – he resembled Oliver Reed. For over a year he tried to poison my pure and innocent Japanese mind with diseased, pagan thoughts and trickery. I did not fall for him. He failed successfully.

Kotaro Sarai
English student to Mr Lynes (apparently)

'In Japan we sometimes have bad dreams, they are called nightmares. In England your dreams will come true.'

My Nightmare in England An A-Z

ENGLAND THROUGH THE EYES OF A BLOODY-MINDED, DEVIANT, XENOPHOBIC JAPANESE VISITOR

Colin Lynes
and Kotaro Sarai

PAN BOOKS

First published 1996 by Pan Books

an imprint of Macmillan Publishers Ltd
25 Eccleston Place, London SW1W 9NF
and Basingstoke

Associated companies throughout the world

ISBN 0 330 35038 2

9 8 7 6 5 4 3 2 1

A CIP catalogue record for this book is available from
the British Library.

Phototypeset by Intype London Ltd
Printed and bound in Great Britain by
MacKays of Chatham plc, Chatham, Kent

Kotaro's dedication

First, I would like to say 'thank you' to my parents. They have fed me and loved me patiently. They bred me to fight for Japan. 'Dad, Mum, I did what you told me to do. I have completed my mission.' Seriously, I'm a nice guy really – in other words a philanthropist. I love everyone, especially people who buy this book.

P.S. Remember Pearl Harbor

Colin's dedication

With thanks to Ros, Rachel and Simon, Sue Seifert, Annie Hudson, Jack Cigman, Peter Cowley, Kay Weller, Tony Nix and Carmel, and Ferhat Engin for their selfless work to preserve an endangered species – love Colin.

Acknowledgement

This book has been produced despite the patient efforts of Teruko Iwanaga and the Euro-Japanese Exchange Foundation to enhance understanding between Japan and the West over the past twenty years.

Special thanks to Simon '10 per cent and the rest in scratch cards' Lynes and Mike Billson (Brain of Botley) for their contributions to the text and inability to take us seriously.

Introduction

Dear Publisher

Colin sent a fax from you to me, so, I read the fax from you. As you probably know, I am quite a usual, typical Japanese businessman and very sane.

In a way, all I said in the book is representative of Japanese people's image of England and the English. In spite of this fact, in your fax you said you 'found *My Nightmare in England* extremely funny'.

Did you insult me and the Japanese people?

Kotaro Sarai

Mr Kotaro Sarai
(on a good day)

A

A, spelt 'Eh?', expresses surprise and confusion.

Example:

> 'Nice to meet you, Mr Sarai.'
> 'Eh?'

Aaaah Soooo / Arsehole

Native speakers expect Japanese to say 'Aaaaah, Soooo'. Say it very slowly, breathing softly but heavily. You are expected to half-close your eyes and move your head up and down in a 13° arc (use a protractor while you practise). You need not contribute anything more to conversation. It replaces listening.

> 'I had a great night last night, Kotaro.'
> 'Aaaah, Soooo.'
> 'We met in the pub.'
> 'Aaaah, Soooo.'
> 'And got to the match just before kick-off.'

'Aaaah, Soooo.'

'Two-nil down at half-time.'

'Aaaah, Soooo.'

When you feel that you are going to vomit with boredom if the conversation continues, slightly change the sound but continue as before.

'Anyway, we turned it round in the second half.'

'Aaare, Soool.'

'Got a winner in the last minute.'

'Aaare, Sool.'

'Got right pissed after, didn't we?'

'Arsehole.'

'What was that you said, Kotaro?'

'Aaaah, Soooo.'

'Funny little bastards, you Japs!'

NB An arsehole is the hole in your bottom – it is a rude word, pronounced asshole in American.

Abstract expressions

These English expressions are usually not based on reality or everyday life. They can mean anything or nothing.

They include:

'Well, well.'

'Quite.'

'Really.'

'Quite, quite.'
'How interesting.'
'Well I never.'
'Ta-ta.'

These words are essential for Japanese speakers. They enable us to continue never-ending conversations automatically.

'So I came off the M25 at junction 7.'
'Quite.'
'The roundabout was packed.'
'Really.'
'So I went back on at junction 9.'
'Well, I never.'
'And drove past junction 10.'
'How interesting.'
'And decided to try junction 12.'
'Quite, quite.'
'There was another jam.'
'A-ha.'
'At junction 12.'
'Well, well.'
'So I decided to turn back.'
'Ta-ta.'

Do not use 'ho-ho' in this way. Ho-ho is an artificial substitute for genuine laughter.

Admitting ignorance

To be quite frank, I haven't understood a word you have said for the past three and a half months.

Alienated

To feel alienated is to feel that you do not belong somewhere or that you are not part of something.

In England you will feel alienated.

Don't worry too much. So do many English.

All right, John?
(pronounced 'Awight')

Used by Englishmen to communicate their friendly feelings to complete strangers in public toilets. The polite response is to stare at the wall in front of you and repeat, 'All right!'

(NB: this phrase is only used when standing.)

Do not try to shake hands.
Do not offer your business card.
Definitely do not say:

'I think you are mistaken. My name is not John. I am from Japan. I apologize for starting World War II. Here is my business card. If you ever visit Japan, you are welcome to come and stay with my family. Thank you for your conversation. I hope we meet again.'

Ants

In England most ants are black. There are very few white ants. Do not step on them. There are also red ants. They bite.
[see: *Economic insects*]

Apparently

Question tags are often used in English (e.g., don't you? have you?, etc).

Example:

'It's hot, isn't it?'

It is difficult to know if this is a question or a statement. If you answer 'apparently' you do not have to think about the problem.

Example:

'You love me, don't you?'
'Apparently . . .'
[see: *If you say so*]

There is also an unchanging question tag pronounced something like 'Noah-min?' I think it may be Chinese.

As you do

English people say this when they believe that what they do is normal.

Example:

'Went to the pub, had a few pints, as you do. Picked up a curry. As you do. Threw it up on the bus, as you do.'

People in England often demand:

'Tell us about a typical day in your life back home.'

I have prepared the following responses:

'I got up at 4.30 a.m. to tell my new joke to our milkman. As you do. I fell asleep again. As you do. I got up again at 4.47 a.m. to tell my new joke to the paperman. As you do. This morning I was quite happy because they both laughed so I decided to go to work. As you do.

'I woke my parents up by attacking them with a Japanese sword. As you do. I had breakfast with my dog to teach him how to use chopsticks. As you do. So far, he hasn't used them well but I never give up. I fell asleep on the train thinking about tomorrow morning's joke. As you do.

'I counted the number of steps from the station to my office. As you do. It was 444 but 4 is an unlucky number in Japan so I decided to go back to the station and do it again. As you do. This time it was 777. I was very glad.

'I worked from 9 a.m. to 5 p.m. In Japan we call this "rather fun". As you do. After 5 p.m. I started counting the steps from my office to the station. It was 444 again. I did not worry – it is a stupid game.

'Went to my local bar. Told today's joke to the barmaid. As you do. Started to worry about tomorrow's joke. As you do.

I got back home around midnight. Apparently.

Avoiding conversation

Speaking English is easy. Problems start when native speakers answer. These are four of the ways of avoiding conversation.

1. Leaving immediately. A useful expression is: 'I must be going. My cat has got diarrhoea.'
2. Persuading the English speaker to leave immediately. A useful expression is: 'Don't let me keep you.'
3. Persuading everyone to leave immediately. A useful expression is: 'I don't want to worry you but I think I can smell gas.'
4. Pretending you have lost your memory.

    Example:

    'Good morning, Mr Sarai.'
    'Who the hell are you? Where's my mum?'
5. Alternatively, you can put your finger in your ears and keep talking.

Example:

'How do you do? Kotaro Sarai. And you. Fine, thank you. Not far from Tokyo. Really, not very often. Boiled eggs. Six months in London. Would you like a cigarette? My company's name is Sarai . . . I like the recession. Here you are. Two nights in Bath. I'd be delighted. I was happy when I was three. I collect toothpaste-tube caps. Very strict. The officers should work alongside the men. How are you, you old bastard, are you still beating your wife? Don't mind if I do, old boy . . .' etc.

With practice, it is possible to continue speaking like this for two or more hours.

Avoiding people

There are over sixty million people in England and it is difficult to avoid all of them.

Places to be alone:

Church pulpits

Crematoriums and cemeteries

Telephone boxes

Public toilets

Cinemas in the afternoon

On tops of trees in a camouflage jacket
Railway tunnels
Centres of roundabouts
London
Refrigerators
Inside washing machines. [You must load your-self from the front. Do not try to enter through the soap-hole.]

Asking for information

Do not be afraid to ask English people for help. Even if you cannot understand their replies, it makes them feel useful. If you use the expression 'Do you happen to know . . .?', native speakers will not feel useless if they do not.

Example:

'Excuse me, do you happen to know why you are wearing my coat?'

B

Bathtime

In Japan we shower first to clean our bodies and then relax in a deliciously hot bath of clean water. Possibly because of water shortages, the British have a bath *or* a shower – it is absolutely forbidden to do both.

Instructions

1. Fill bath. No more than 10 centimetres (remember, water is precious).
2. Place small yellow plastic duck on the surface of the water.
3. Sit upright and wash your body with soap. If you are washing your hair it is necessary to kneel and put your head in the water.
4. Lie back and soak your body in the dirty water (no more than fifteen minutes).
5. Get out of the bath and then rub the dirty water off your body with a clean towel until you feel hot and the towel is dirty.
6. Clean and dry duck. If the duck is clean, you are clean. OK?

Beaming and nodding

A beaming smile is a bright and happy smile. To nod is to move your head down and up quickly to indicate 'yes'. By combining a beaming smile and energetic nodding it is possible to continue a conversation that you do not understand. If you suspect a joke laugh out loud.

Bilge

This word is used to express strong disagreement.

Example:

'Great film, wasn't it!'
'Bilge.'

Birth

English people are born regularly. In fact there is a saying in England, 'There is one born every minute.' This means five hundred and twenty-five thousand six hundred native speaking idiots are born every year. Mainly, they form queues at bus stops and outside football stadiums.

Blood groups

In Japan we all know our blood groups. British people do not. I suspect they may be −3°C.

Bloody Nips!

In World War II the Japanese were called 'Nips'. This word suggests a bloodthirsty little yellow slitty-eyed Japanese not quite human being.

The word derives from Nippon. Compare:

Nippon . . . a Nip
Scotland . . . a Scot
Germany . . . a Germ?
England . . . an Eng?

The expression 'There's a bit of a nip in the air this morning' does not mean that there is a small segment of a bloodthirsty little yellow slitty-eyed Japanese not quite human being flying in the sky. It means that it is somewhat cold.

Practise this phrase on strangers at bus stops on cold mornings. Enjoy their horror and confusion.

Alternatively, at meetings, puff air from your

bottom, smile sweetly and say: 'There seems to be a bit of a nip in the air this morning.' As they are choking in their coffee, you must explain. 'It is a Japanese joke; my grandfather from Hokkaido told it to me before he was executed. I'm glad you enjoy our traditional Japanese humour. You are kind!'

Blowing your nose

In Japan, blowing your nose in public causes embarrassment. In England you can happily blow your nose, in any place, at any time, in front of anyone – except when making love to a new partner.

Boiled eggs and Marmite soldiers

A boiled egg is an egg which has been boiled, but not a lot. Marmite soldiers are thin strips of toast spread with butter and Marmite. Using fingers, 'the soldiers' are dipped into the egg and then eaten. It is a very messy and time-consuming way of eating an egg.

Ninety-nine per cent of native speakers were

persuaded by their mothers that this combination is delicious.

English people believe that anyone who likes boiled eggs and Marmite soldiers is warm-hearted and not foreign.

If you want to persuade people in England that you are sweet and kind you must lie and say, 'My favourite food is a boiled egg with Marmite soldiers.'

Example:

'What do you miss most from Japan?'
'Boiled eggs and Marmite soldiers.'

Bored rigid

Often in England you will be so bored that your body will not respond to the messages from your brain. You will be unable to move. To avoid this embarrassing situation you must keep some part of your body moving.

Practise at home. Sit in front of a mirror and concentrate on your ears. They will move up and down. It is called 'wiggling your ears'. If your nose moves it is 'twitching', not wiggling. If anything else moves, it is a symptom of sexual frustration.

Bricks

Most English homes are made of small red objects called bricks. Without bricks most English people would be homeless. Although bricks are essential to British society, they are not suitable as gifts – even if wrapped Japanese style.

The Bridge on the River Kwai

In Japan this film is an anti-war film. In England, it is a war film about British defiance in the face of Japanese cruelty. Tell English people how much you enjoyed it. You will then understand the meaning of the expression 'gob-smacked'.

Bugger

Originally the word 'bugger' described an unusual sexual activity between men. Nowadays, the word has many different meanings:

1. Go away!

   Example:

   > Shop assistant: 'Can I help you?'
   > Kotaro Sarai: 'Bugger off!'

2. Something to say to yourself when you are disappointed. For example, if you discover too late that there is no toilet paper in the toilet: 'Bugger it!'

3. A warm greeting to an old friend.

   Example:

   > 'Hello, you old bugger.'

4. 'Bugger up.'
   When something is buggered up, it is spoiled or damaged in some way.

   Example:

   > 'Thank you for phoning, you've buggered up my entire day.'

[NB: 'Bugger me!' is an expression of surprise, *not* an invitation.]

Business cards

The exchange of business cards is a very serious ceremony in Japan. English people do not understand this and will insult you by not even looking at your card before tucking it in their back pocket.

You will feel insulted but you can get your revenge by spitting on *their* business card, tossing it over your left shoulder and saying, 'In Japan, we do this for luck.'

Button / bottom

Japanese speakers cannot hear the difference between these two words. It does not matter.

'Did you enjoy the wedding, Kotaro?'

'Very lovely, especially the pretty little flowers in the bottom holes.'

C

Cannibalism

Cannibals are people who eat people (hot or cold). There have been few cannibals in England since the sixteenth century and it is almost unnecessary to worry about being eaten. There are far more frightening things in Britain – such as roundabouts [see *Roundabouts*].

Do not worry if native speakers say, 'We are having people for dinner tonight.' It means that they are inviting, not eating.

Chance would be a fine thing

Life is not pleasant in the UK. English people make it worse by trying to be positive and cheerful. Used as an antidote, a way of expressing your deep feeling of hopelessness and envy is, 'Chance would be a fine thing'.

Example:

'Did you meet any nice English people last night?'

'Chance would be a fine thing.'

Chatting up the birds

To chat up a bird is to talk to a woman in a friendly way with the hope of beginning a romantic relationship.

Example:

'Hello there, where are you from?'
'Really?'
'Would you like a drink?'

The Kotaro Sarai approach is more direct:

'Good evening, for the past eight months, seven days, three hours and twenty minutes I have had an election. Help me please, thank you, *domo*. I have decided to love you. Do you have children? No? Would you like one of mine? Are you sure? Thank you. Have a nice day.'

Chin-chin

English people sometimes say this, meaning 'cheers', when they are drinking alcohol. In Japanese, your 'chinchin' is your penis (see *Willy*).
　'Chin-chin, Kotaro.'
Do not react by looking down at your trouser zip. Smile and reply
　'Plick-plick.'
　or
　'Pronker-pronker.'
　[NB: 'chin up' is *not* a sexual invitation.]

Christianity

Christians believe that Jesus Christ gave his life to atone for the sins of mankind. Many Japanese have committed suicide to lift blame from their countrymen. Could He have been . . .?

Colonel Bogey's March

In kindergarten in Japan we did our morning exercises to this jolly tune. When you are feeling lost and trapped in England, hold your head up, swing your arms and whistle 'Colonel Bogey' as you walk along the streets.

English people become alarmed and confused when I do this. I don't know why.

Couch potato

Couch potatoes are grown in the north-east of England, near to the Scottish border.

Creating a bad atmosphere

It is easy to poison the atmosphere at social occasions in England by showing great enthusiasm for any of the following:

Japan's economic growth since World War II

Japan's whaling industry

The beauty of ivory

The importance of chopsticks made of teak or mahogany

The superiority of Japanese technology

The military value of surprise attacks

Hanging

In English, the verb 'crop up' is used when problems or difficulties happen unexpectedly.

Example:

'Hello, Barbara, I hadn't expected you to crop up tonight . . .'

D

Death

English people die – regularly. In this way, they are quite similar to Japanese people.

Delicious

When you are offered a plate of food in England, to be polite, look at it carefully and say, 'Delicious', *before you taste it*. It is too late afterwards.
[see: *How is your food?*]

Depression

Depression is a feeling of unhappiness, loneliness and hopelessness that lasts for a long time. In England you will feel depressed. When I feel depressed I sit under a willow tree beside a cool river and imagine that I am strangling a duck.

Disparagement

Beware when the English are polite and kind to you! It can be a tactic to make you feel inferior. In the English language this form of personal attack is called disparagement. The words may be sweet, but their delayed action is designed to humiliate you.

Example:

'Oh, Kotaro, you are so sweet.' ('Sweet' means pathetic, insignificant, pitiable)

'I'd really love to talk to you more, but ...' (means 'Go *away*')

'I'm sure Barbara will look after you . . .' (means 'You are not capable of looking after yourself, you little yellow wimp')

You must retaliate instantly:

With an innocent smile, clear your throat and say softly and sweetly, but persistently: 'What *exactly* do you mean by that?'

If the native speaker explains, he has lost. If he does not explain, he has lost.

Disparagement can be fun!

'I've started learning Japanese, Kotaro!'
'I'm so sorry to hear that.'

or

'You English are so clever with those knives and forks. We Japanese have never really got beyond chopsticks.'

or

'I don't get much attention but I'm sure I don't deserve it.'

Don't ask

If you reply 'Don't ask' to a question it means that to reply to the question would cause you unnecessary suffering by reminding you of experiences that you wish to forget.

Example:

'How was your trip?'
'Don't ask.'

or

'I'm sorry to trouble you but would you mind awfully if I opened the window?'
'Don't ask.'

Don't mention it

English people reply 'Don't mention it' to a thank-you. So never say thank you to them. You can use this phrase yourself.

Example:

'Thank you for leaving, Kotaro.'
'Don't mention it.'

Another possibility is:

'Kotaro, you are a deviant xenophobic slitty-eyed wanker.'
'Don't mention it.'

Do you know who I am?

English people say this when they want you to believe that they are important. They are only pretending that they cannot remember. You can: Lift both your arms straight and parallel in the air and shout 'Banzai!' Or reply innocently and helpfully:

'No, have you forgotten?'

'To be honest, I have lost your business card, sorry.'

'No I don't, but I remember when we met for the first time.'

'Do you mind if I change the subject?'

Dream on, you sad bastard!

This informal expression can be understood as meaning, 'I am very sorry but I cannot agree with your suggestion.'

We Japanese find it uncouth to say 'No' directly. This expression is invaluable for communicating with less sensitive native speakers, who might otherwise miss the point.

Example:

> 'Kotaro, I'd love to visit you in Japan.'
> 'Really?' (= Oh no!)
> 'Can I stay at your home?'
> 'I'll see what I can do.' (= No way!)
> 'Great, I'll be arriving on May 10th.'
> *'Dream on, you sad bastard!'*

or

> 'Your round, Kotaro.'
> *'Dream on, you sad bastard!'*

[NB: A useful response to the phrase 'Your round' is 'No I'm not.' While they are confused by this, someone else, with luck, will have bought the drinks.]

E

Echoing

Echoing is a method of continuing conversations that you are not interested in or do not understand. You simply repeat the last part of the speaker's sentence.

Oxford is a famous city.
. . . a famous city . . .
It has a tradition of learning.
. . . of learning . . .
Many famous people have studied at the university.
. . . at the university . . .
Have you been to Oxford before?
. . . before?

or

Life is but a melancholy flower?
. . . Butter? Melon? Cauliflower???

Economic insects

English people sometimes call us Japanese 'economic insects'. I have counted my legs. There are only two.

Elation

Elation is a feeling of great happiness. I have never felt elated in England.

English bottoms

English bottoms are generally much larger than Japanese bottoms, unless you are a sumo wrestler. Consequently, English toilets are large and round (like their eyes) while Japanese toilets are small and oval (like our eyes).

It is essential (especially on aeroplanes) to hold on to the toilet seat tightly with both hands. The safety distance for flushing is 1.26 metres.

I personally always carry a piece of string to use as a measure.

Er and Um

We Japanese mainly think in silence (an occasional hissing intake of breath is acceptable). The English make the sounds 'er' and 'um' to reassure the listener that they are alive. You must practise on hotel receptionists and customs officials to become perfect. Each 'er' or 'um' must last not less than 4.92 seconds.

'How do you spell your name, Mr Sarai?'

'S . . . ummmmmmmmmmmmmmmmmmm

A . . . errrrrrrrrrrrrrrrrrrrrrrrrrrrrrrrrrrrrrrrrrrrrrrrr

R . . . ummmmmmmmmmmmmmmmmmmmmm

A . . . errrrrrrrrrrrrrrrrrrrrrrrrrrrrrrrrrrrrrrrrrrrrrrrr'

'Is "I" the letter you're looking for, Mr Sarai?'

'I didn't know I'd lost one. No, don't tell me, I'll start again.

K . . . errrrrrrrrrrrrrrrrrrrrrrrrrrrr . . .'

Escalators

Like Japanese, the English drive on the left. Unlike Japanese, the English go up and down escalators on the right. Do not worry about this lack of consistency – they do not know better.

By facing in the opposite direction to the commuters, you can either look up appealingly while counting their nasal hairs, or look down unhappily while dribbling on their bald patches.

Either way you can practise creating Japanese Haiku on the theme of dandruff.

F

Falling asleep in public

In Japan it is natural to fall asleep on trains. It is safe, because the crime rate is very low in Japan. In England falling asleep in public, without a teddy bear, is a sign of a weak character.

If you want to fall asleep on the train, you must make an announcement to the other passengers:

'My name is Kotaro Sarai. My company is Sarai. I am Japanese. This is my teddy bear, his name is Sumo. I am soon going to fall asleep. Do not worry, in Japan there is no dishonour. I will not lose face. Thank you for your attention. If you have any questions, I'll be pleased to answer them when I wake up. Thank you. Good night.'

Feminism

In Japan, women are humble in public and bossy in private. In England, some women are bossy in private *and* public. They are called feminists.

Fundamental differences between Japan and Britain

There are not enough vending machines in the UK. [see: *Vending machines*]

G

Gap fillers

Gap fillers are used when there is a silence in the conversation and you need something to say.

Examples:

'I wouldn't pay for sex, would you?

'What a lovely pine shelf! How long did it take you to put it up?'

'I don't like men with big bushy moustaches, do you?'

'. . . well, anyway.'

Get a life, Kotaro!

I tried Harrods but the manager said, 'We don't stock Japanese lives; there's no demand.'

Giving directions

This language is almost completely unnecessary. Native speakers would not dream of asking Japanese people for directions.

God

Western people link their idea of God with religion. This explains a lot.

Going down with the ship

In the Royal Navy, there is a tradition that the honourable captain remains with his ship until it sinks to the bottom of the sea. As this happens, he should stand to attention and salute the British flag. This is an English imitation of Japanese hara-kiri. [see *Hara-kiri*].

Why do they do this? It is a waste of manpower and a source of sea pollution.

Gravy

Gravy is a substance made of animal juice, fat, flour and left-over vegetable water. The English pour it over their food. It is very sticky and difficult to remove . . .

Hairy women have hearts

Women in the UK are not all aggressive and competitive but you need to be careful. For example, you can say to a woman, 'I like your top,' but you cannot say, 'I like your bottom.' If you are a

Japanese man you are expected to be rich. Even feminists will allow you to pay the bill.

Halt, who goes there?

English soldiers shout this when approached in the dark by menacing strangers. English people are strange and menacing. Use this expression if someone knocks at the door of the toilet where you are hiding from the hairy ones.

Knock, knock.

'Halt, who goes there?'

'It's only me, Barbara.'

'I do not know that one.'

'Are you OK, Kotaro?'

'Leave me alone, we Japanese have small anuses.'

[NB: English soldiers also shout 'Friend or foe?' (enemy). You need not ask this question. You will have no friends in England.]

Handshakes

At home we Japanese normally do not touch strangers – when we greet each other we bow. It is a simple ritual. In the West a complicated ceremony has evolved: it is called the 'handshake'.

Many Japanese are confused by this strange desire for immediate physical contact with strangers of the same sex. There are four vital elements of this ceremony to remember at all times:

1. Not too firm, not too soft. (Practise by crushing beer cans.)
2. Not too long, not too short. (You must let go.)

3. Not too wet, not too dry. (You can use a hairdryer.)

4. Do it once only to each person.

Either

Practise on yourself until it feels comfortable

Or

Perform the hand movement at a safe distance from the native speaker (no closer than 1.379 metres) before they have a chance to touch you. I call this the 'Sarai Airshake'.

Or

Put your thumb to your nose and waggle your fingers.

Hara-kiri

In Japan, the British have a reputation for being blonde and eating bacon and eggs every day for breakfast. In Britain, the Japanese have a reputation for hara-kiri.

Most English people do not understand the meaning of hara-kiri. Hara-kiri is a very special type of suicide where it is necessary to slit open your stomach with a sharp knife before a helper cuts off your head. The 'helper' must be patient. Kamikaze pilots could not possibly commit hara-kiri because they were too busy trying to kill themselves.

Privately, you will be asked, 'Why do you do it? It is a waste of life.' Possible answers include:

'We Japanese just love it. If I have a chance I'd like to try it once. It's just like bungee jumping.'
'Suicides have been rationed in Japan. We are only allowed one each.'
'It looks good on a CV.'
'Whose life is it anyway?'
'It runs in the family.'
'It's our way of "going down with the ship".'

Have you made any plans for the weekend?

When people say this to me, I know they want me to go away.

For example:

'Have you made any plans for the weekend?'
'Yes, I'm staying here with you.'

Heat

Some summer days in England are very hot and generally there is no air-conditioning. Put a large bag of frozen peas on your head.

Hello/Harrow

When we Japanese say 'hello' it sounds like 'Harrow' to the natives. When Japanese visitors arrive at Heathrow, our first word in English is often 'hello' to a taxi driver. This is why so many Japanese are living in Harrow.

Here you are

When English people hand you something, they may say, 'Here you are.' Or they may say, 'There you are.' You will not know *where* you are.

Hobbies

English people will often ask you about your hobbies and interests. It helps if you prepare a list.

Example:

1. Shopping at Harrods
2. Shaving my forehead and trimming nasal hair
3. Standing on windowsills
4. Pretending to be dead
5. Following closely behind learner drivers

Hogwash

This is another useful word to express strong disagreement [see: *Bilge*]. Hogwash is a food for pigs.

Example:

'We English have a lot in common with the Japanese.'
'Hogwash!'

Homestays

When you are in England you may stay in an English family home. This gives you a wonderful opportunity to understand the full meaning of alienation [see *Alienated*]. The most useful phrase is: 'Excuse me, I am very busy.' This gives you the opportunity to escape to your bedroom and feel sad.

[NB: make friends with the bedroom wallpaper on your first night.]

How are things?

What are these things? Everywhere in England there are things. Things are good, things are bad, things change, things look up but don't look down. Which things are they talking about?

How are you?

English people continually ask, 'How are you?' You must always answer 'Fine', even if your mother has just died. A useful expression is 'Mustn't grumble', which means 'I am forbidden to complain'.

Do not confuse with 'How do you do?', to which the answer is 'How do you do?'

How dare you!

'How dare you!' expresses violent anger. Even if you are not angry you can escape unwanted situations by shouting: 'How dare you!' walking out and slamming the door.

Example:

'It's your round?'
'How dare you!'

How is your food?

In England in homes and restaurants while you are trying to eat you are regularly asked the strange question, 'How is your food?' You need not become suspicious, it is a British custom. To be polite, it is necessary to answer. If you prepare a list of answers it is unnecessary to think before you reply.

Example:

> Monday: 'Interesting!'
> Tuesday: 'Quite interesting!'
> Wednesday: 'Rather interesting!'
> Thursday: 'Really quite interesting!'
> Friday: 'Really rather interesting!'
> Saturday: 'Satisfactory!'
> Sunday: 'There's nothing like a traditional roast!'

Alternatively, you can answer comprehensively:

'The colours are dark brown, light green and off-white. The sausages are surrounded by potatoes. They may be afraid that their territory may be occupied by potatoes. The cabbage looks quite apathetic. It might have been boiled for too long. It needs rest. In my opinion, it should be against the law to serve sausages for dinner. They are a breakfast food. We should expel them to maintain harmony. The sausage on the left looks under the weather. I know why. He has been bullied by the other sausages. They deserve punishment. I'll prick them with your fork. Pass me your fork quickly! Don't hesitate! We must do it now! Wait! The potatoes are whispering. Be quiet! Listen to them. What are they talking about? They want to know how you are . . . How are you?'

You will not be asked again!

You can also say, 'I've had a lot on my plate recently.' This expression is not remotely connected to food and means that you have been experiencing many problems recently.

Humbergers

The English cannot spell *'humbergers'*. They spell it *'hamburgers'*.

I

I can't quite put my finger on it

Use this expression when you are unsure.

Example:

'How are you today?'
'I can't quite put my finger on it.'

I can't wait

Very useful phrase to express lack of enthusiasm.

Example:

'This is a traditional English recipe.'
[In a tired voice] 'I can't wait.'

Also

'Would you like to see my holiday snaps?'
[In a tired voice] 'I can't wait.'

I don't expect I shall be here much longer

This suggests that you are going to die soon.

Example:

'How long are you staying in England?'
'I don't expect I shall be here much longer.'

I don't mind if I do

Use this expression when you are offered food or drink. It will surprise and amuse English people. I don't know why. It seems, possibly, to mean 'It is not important to me if I do', or perhaps 'Do not worry if I do'. Do it anyway.

Example:

'Would you like a Twiglet?'
'Don't mind if I do.'

I hear you

'I hear you' means I can hear the sound of your voice but I am not listening to what you are saying.

Example:

'Please stop doing that, Mr Sarai; it's rude.'
'I hear you.'

I spy

In England there is a children's game called 'I spy'. One child picks out an object in the room and gives the other children the first letter of the name of the object. The other children have to guess the object. It is very boring. You can destroy conversation at native speaker social occasions by insisting on playing this game.

Example:

'I spy with my slitty little eye something beginning with 'L'.'
'OK, that's enough. What is it, Kotaro?'
'Ladiator.'

I wouldn't disagree with you

An expression of diplomatic disagreement with someone who is bigger than you (e.g. a large feminist).

If that's what you think, you've got another think coming

An expression of violent disagreement with someone who is smaller than you (e.g. a small feminist).
[see *Feminism*]

If you have any questions, don't hesitate to ask

Kotaro Sarai: 'When are you leaving?'

If you say so

An expression of tired agreement with someone who is very boring.

Example:

'You're looking well.'
'If you say so.'

or

'Your English is improving.'
'If you say so.'

or

'What a beautiful sunset.'
'If you say so.'

or

'Tomorrow is Wednesday, isn't it?'
'If you say so.'

I'll get them in

This means 'I will buy the drinks'. Do not confuse with 'I will get them off', which means 'I will remove my or your clothes'.

Example:

'Sit down; I'll get them off.'

I'll have your guts for garters

This means 'I will use the contents of your stomach to hold up my socks/tights'. It is a threat.

I'll see what I can do

This is a very confusing expression, which clearly means 'no' to the Japanese, but English people deviously use it to say 'yes'. Be careful, especially if you are discussing finance.

In a way

'In a way' is a useful expression for avoiding saying anything.

Example:

'Did you enjoy the film?'
'In a way ...'

[see: *Apparently.*]

Inscrutable

English people say Japanese people are inscrutable. They are saying we are weird. But if the Japanese are inscrutable, therefore the English should be scrutable. I personally have found them impossible to scrute.

Insiders / Outsiders

In England there are two types of people, 'insiders' and 'outsiders'. Insiders are part of society, outsiders are not. We Japanese are inside-out. I am not sure what this means but it is better than being upside-down.

Interrupting

We Japanese are often too polite to interrupt when someone is speaking. A traditional English method of interrupting is to say in a clear and loud voice, *'Shut up and listen to me.'*

Is anyone sitting there?

If you are sitting next to any empty seat, British people will ask you, 'Is anyone sitting there?' They are not blind. They are, in fact, asking for permission to sit next to you. To refuse your permission tactfully, put your hand on the seat and say, 'It's still warm, I think she may be returning.'

Is the Pope a Catholic?

We use this expression when the answer to a question is obvious and clear. The question itself is, therefore, totally unnecessary.

Example:

Are you looking forward to going back to Japan?
Is the Pope a Catholic?

[NB: the Pope *is* a Catholic!]

Similarly:

Does a bear shit in the woods?

It depends what you mean by

Repeating this phrase in conversations can make conversations longer and irritates the native speaker.

Example:

'Do you like English food?'
'It depends what you mean by like.'
'By like, I mean enjoy.'
'Well, it depends on what you mean by mean.'

It's a cross between X and Y

People will often ask you unimaginative questions about Japanese culture. Do not worry – they are not really interested and you can answer with the above phrase.

Example:

'What's so special about eating raw fish, anyway, Kotaro?'

'Eating raw fish is a cross between human flesh and chewing condoms.'

[NB: try to link two completely dissimilar items. The native speaker will soon get confused and give up.]

It's a moot point

Sometimes you are asked questions but you do not want to answer. Most English people do not know the exact meaning of 'It's a moot point', so they stop asking the question.

Example:

'How are you getting on with your wife?'
'It's a moot point.'

It's better than . . .

You will often be asked for your opinion of your experiences in England. Many useful expressions begin with 'It's better than . . .'

'It's better than a slap in the face with a dead fish.'

'It's better than sleeping with a dead policeman.'

'It's better than a plate of cold sick.'

For example:

'Enjoying the ride, Mr Sarai?'
'It's better than a poke in the stick with a pointed eye.'

K

Keeping a diary

Keep a record of your misery. One day revenge
may be possible.

Extract from the diary of Kotaro Sarai:

5/9/94

My Arrival

Today, I am not happy. I arrived at Heathrow. I kept
close to a group of Japanese tourists, I was trying
to pretend I was a member. The first person I met
was an Indian. I thought I was in Delhi by mistake.
The airport looked dangerous. I really wanted to go
to the toilet, but I had to suppress the natural urge
because of my suitcase. To have a pee, I would have
had to let go of the handle. I was sure it would
have been stolen. Where am I? Who am I? Why
me?

VJ Day

Today, I decided personally to make a humble apology to as many English people as possible for starting World War II. I got up at four o'clock in the morning and followed the milkman. After he delivered the milk, I knocked on the doors. People did not seem pleased to see me.

21 Beech Avenue
'Good morning. This is your milk. I'm so sorry to crop up suddenly. Do you happen to know what we, the Japanese, did in 1941? We were very bad people. You may not have noticed but I'm sure you want me to apologize for that. Can you understand what I said?'

The lady looked confused. I tried again.

'We . . . Japan . . . very bad . . . not good people . . . anyway we changed ourselves. Ah . . . you . . . I . . . friends . . . you good . . . me good . . . happy . . . sorry to be nuisance . . . Bye.'

She shut the door suddenly. Five minutes later, I knocked again.

'Sorry, one thing. I forgot to apologize. I'm sorry . . . sorry. Have a nice day!'

She said, 'You are not our regular milkman.'

23 Beech Avenue
I decided to try a new tactic.

'Hello, how do you do? My name is Kotaro Sarai.

I'm from Japan. You must be angry with me because my grandad used to work at the Japanese prison during World War II. He might have done something terrible to your father but he didn't do that on purpose. Don't misunderstand him. Basically, he was a nice guy. Anyway that's all in the past. He died two years ago.'

The woman stared at the milk bottle in my hand. (It was cold and slippery.) Then she stared at me. Again, she stared at the milk bottle. I became irritated, my fingers were cold.

'Why didn't you come to his funeral? Why are you so heartless? I don't want to talk to you any more. I don't think we will meet again. Bye. Have a nice day!'

She said, 'You are not our regular milkman.'

25 Beech Avenue

I decided to try a more direct approach.

'Good morning. I'm not your regular milkman. I'm Japanese. My name is Kotaro Sarai. In 1941, I, Kotaro Sarai, attacked Pearl Harbor and started World War II. I'm lying. But I'm sorry. We all do silly things when we are young. There is one born every minute. I wasn't born yesterday.'

She said, 'When is our regular milkman coming back?'

I looked around me, there was a church in the street (churches are buildings with crosses on the roof). There was a man wearing a long dress, he looked me down and up. He was not expecting milk but something else. 'Can I help you?' he said.

'Thank you, many native speakers do not want to hear. They only want milk. My name is Kotaro Sarai. I was born in the Saitama Prefecture. Never mind, it is near Tokyo. Would you believe it? I started World War II. You don't, never mind. Neither do I, but I must apologize. We haven't really been introduced.'

The man in a dress sat me in a wardrobe with a door in the side and closed the door. I thought, 'Good, I am a prisoner now, I can suffer happily.'

A small window opened in the darkness and I heard a voice. 'What is it, my son?'

I said, 'You are not my father. My father has a Japanese accent and does not wear a dress. Mustn't grumble, I will call you "Daddy".'

The man started to breathe heavily, he smelt of boiled eggs and Marmite soldiers. I spoke quickly. 'Daddy, somebody started World War II. He is not here but I am. (He was not a milkman.) I must be punished severely. My name is Kotaro Sarai. It is too dark for you to read my business card but I will post it later, so sorry. I must buy a luminous one. I promise. Love means never having to say you're sorry. Did you see the film? We needed subtitles, of course. I do not love you.'

The voice said, 'You are disturbed, my son. Say ten Hail Marys and go in peace.'

I was confused, I did not know any native

speakers called Mary. It is a woman's name. I said, 'Why are you wearing a dress?'

He said, 'It is a frock, my son.' (Later I looked in my dictionary. 'A frock is a summer dress'.)

I said, 'Thanks, Dad, but just one thing, don't be formal! Call me Kotaro.' and left the church. The light hurt my contact lenses. I was dazzled. That's a good word.

A woman with long blonde hair and light in her clear blue eyes smiled at me. I said, 'Hello, Mary.'

She said, 'My name is not Mary, you are weird. Piss off! You are not our regular milkman.'

Kindly take your hand off my knee

If a stranger puts his hand on your knee you may decide to use this expression [also see *Oi!*]. If someone says it to you, stand up, bow and say, 'I'm sorry, sorry. I am ashamed, please punish me if you are not busy.'

Kotaro's history of the English Crown

Like all Japanese, I am fascinated by the English Royal Family, so I did some research. The last all-English king I could find was in 1066. Then they were all Frenchmen called Norman for a long time and even after that there was as much French or Welsh or Scottish blood in them as English. When these ran out, the country started again, with a German, who didn't speak English, called George, married to a German.

Their son was a German called George who married a German and had a son called Fred who married a German but was killed playing cricket so the crown went to his son. . . .

George, who married a German, had a son called George who married an English-woman secretly but this wasn't approved of, so he married a German. However, he had no heir, and neither did his brother (William). Who was married to a German, so these two I discard.

Next came his niece, the famous Queen Victoria who was named after the railway station. Her father was the son of the George before the last one and her mother was . . . yes. She married a

German, but one of her best friends was a Scotsman. She had lots of children who married all over Europe, including several Germans.

Her eldest son was called Edward and married a Danish princess, but to make up for this they had a son called George who married a German.

At this point World War I occurred, and Germans became unfashionable. The next king, Edward again, wanted to marry an American!!! but this was going much too far, so he resigned. He was replaced by his brother, George again. However, his wife was Scottish, so the present queen Elizabeth II does not have as much German blood as her ancestors. Her husband, Prince Philip, Duke of Edinburgh, was officially Greek but with Danish, German and Russian blood and is another descendant of the English(?) Queen Victoria (see above).

Thus, Prince Charles is a mixture of German, Danish, Greek, Scottish and Russian blood, at least (I forgot the Hungarian). As everyone knows, he married an English lady, with results not necessarily to his advantage.

Perhaps he should have found a nice Japanese girl.

L and R

It is absolutely impossible for Japanese people to pronounce L and R properly. This is not a problem, I have two tactics:

1. *Do not practise pronunciation.* Just ignore the difference. If English people insist on correcting your pronunciation you can get your revenge by repeating the phrase, 'He who raughs rast raughs rongest,' for ten or fifteen minutes at breakfast time every day. (Thirty minutes at weekends.)

2. *Structure your life. Do not visit* Rondon, Reeds or Leading or Riverpool.
   Do not travel to Lussia, Lwanda or Puerto Lico.
   Do not make friends with a Lobert, Lichard, Lachel, Loger or a Barbala.
   Change your address and move to a street or an avenue, *not* a load.
   Do not eat reeks, laddishes, labbit, ramb or in lestaurants.
   Never fall in rove.
   Never listen to Elic Crapton.

M

My hat / my foot

An obscure form of irony; so obscure that no native speaker knows why they use this. When used by a foreigner it will shock them into a state of silent disbelief, giving you a good opportunity to leave the room. Simply repeat part of the sentence and add, 'My foot,' or 'My hat.'

Example:

'That's a lovely tie.'
'Lovely, my hat!'

'That's a lovely hat.'
'Lovely, my foot!'

'Is that a hat?'
'Hat, my hat!'

'What lovely boots.'
'Boots, my foot, lovely, my hat, my boots.'

Don't worry if your English victim seems confused. It serves them right.

N

Ner, ner-ni, ner, ner . . .

Unpleasant English children use this phrase to express their happiness at other English children's unhappiness.

For example:

'I've got a new bike, you haven't, ner, ner-ni, ner, ner.'

'You failed your test. Ner, ner-ni, ner, ner.'

I feel this expression is very satisfying:

'England's in recession. Ner, ner-ni, ner, ner.'

'The NIKKEI index is up again. Ner, ner-ni, ner, ner.'

No man is an island

English people like to show they are highly educated by quoting poetry. This quotation means that nobody is alone. If you are Japanese in England, this is not true. Do not worry. Remember, 'It is *their* island.'

No reason

'English people will often ask different questions that begin with the word 'Why?' All these questions need not be answered if you use the phrase 'no reason'.

Example:

'Why are you taking off your trousers?'
'No reason.'

'Why do the Japanese kill so many whales?'
'No reason.'

'Why are you so short?
'No reason.'

Noodles

I cannot face another day without real Japanese noodles.

Now and then

In Japan we are taught that 'now' means 'at *this* time' and 'then' means 'at *that* time'. When I first arrived at Gatwick Airport, the customs officer began by saying, 'Now then, Mr Sarai, what is the purpose of your visit?'

O

Obituary columns

The recent deaths of native speakers are recorded daily in the obituary columns of the newspapers.

On Sunday afternoons drinking a pina colada, I review my collection to analyse how they died. Sometimes I feel pleased. Sometimes I feel envious. Native speakers call this 'having mixed feelings'.

Oi!

'Oi!' in English means 'Oi!' in Japanese.

P

Patriotism

Patriotism is love of your country. The English love patriotic songs. I like to join in but when I begin singing 'Rand of Hop and Guroly' they all stop.

Pearl Harbor

To avoid disagreements, you must apologize, 'So sorry, Pearl Harbor was very bad manners. We should have knocked.'

Peeled plum tomatoes

To check that the residents of a house are truly English, check the kitchen cupboard. There will be a small but sacred space filled with dusty, dented tins of Peeled Plum Tomatoes. It is a form of shrine. They are believed to be provisions for the after-life. This superstition derives from Egypt.

Personal space

When English people are talking they stand much closer than is normal in Japan.

If you feel uncomfortable, either:

1. Stoop and roll your eyes anticlockwise. It is better to roll one eye anticlockwise, the other clockwise. This is difficult. This needs training.

or

2. Close your eyes tight and wish they would go away.

or

3. Practise bleeding from your nose while keeping a smile on your face.

Politics

People of the Far West expect us people of the Far East to understand their political problems. Save time by preparing your answers:

'What is the Japanese view on the Irish question, Kotaro?'

'In High School, we learn the capital is Belfast.'

or

'Argentina should never have invaded.'

Again

'Where did Japan stand on the Gulf War, Kotaro?'

'In Japan, we understand the importance of golf in the business world. We practise whenever possible and there are many golf courses. Bombing raids are not considered necessary.'

or

'I would like to apologize for the Japanese attitude and lack of participation in the Gulf crisis. This was due to a typing error. So sorry.'

PS. Margaret Thatcher does not seem to me a typical English person.

Prisoners of war

Do not mention the slave trade.

Q

Quoting

If you are completely lost in a conversation take a deep breath and quote a Japanese proverb. For example: 'In Japan we say, ' 'Dust even if it piles grows into mountain'.' In this way you can remain confident and superior while the native speaker will feel confused and inferior.

This technique prevents the conversation from continuing.

R

Radiate disapproval

English people radiate disapproval to make you feel uncomfortable and guilty. Often you will not know what you have done wrong.

Native speakers have difficulty making a noise eating soup and one of the easiest ways of causing English people to radiate disapproval is to suck soup Japanese style with a happy 'sszzsssszzzsss'.

[NB: The nearest English translation of 'sszzsssszzzsss' is 'mmm, yum yum'.

Removing shoes

Like domestic animals, shoes share their lives with the family in the UK. This is why shoes manufactured under the name of Hush Puppies are so popular in England. It is forbidden to take off your shoes when you enter an English home. If you feel uncomfortable wearing shoes in the home, you must buy yourself a pair of wellington boots, also known as wellies. Wellies are long black or green rubber boots specially designed for Land Rover owners. Traditionally, wellies are permitted to be removed when you enter a home, as a sign of respect for the visitor's financial status.

'Leave your wellies in the hall' is a well-known English phrase.

If you cannot avoid having English guests, shouting this phrase from a distance, as they arrive, may deter them.

Rice pudding

Japan is a rice culture. England is a potato culture. The English, however, are cruel to rice. They do a terrible, unmentionable thing to rice – it is called rice pudding.

Revenge is possible. Serve your English guests potatoes cooked in milk and sugar for two hours, as a dessert.

Remember to say:

'I thought you'd like it; it is a special treat in Japan. Another helping? Never mind, I'll save you some to take home. You are looking pale.'

[NB: 'To get your just desserts' is a form of revenge, like saying 'It serves you right'. The English seem to associate food with punishment. Dinner in

England is a death sentence. If you receive an invitation to dinner, immediately send back a note saying little green men from Mars are holding you hostage; but they will release you at 3 o'clock if a hamburger and french fries are left on your doorstep.]

Rigor mortis

Rigor mortis is a stiffening of a body after death. You will experience this at roundabouts and when talking to English feminists [see: *Feminism*].

Roundabouts

In Japan, we have traffic lights. Roundabouts give bored English drivers an opportunity to glimpse death.

Do not shit yourself unnecessarily. Here are two Sarai strategies.

1. Wait in a layby until a learner driver approaches. Follow round closely behind, beeping your horn and flashing your lights.

2. Shut your eyes and drive round and round as fast as you can. There is no law against this!

[NB: 'a roundabout way of doing things' is not necessarily suicidal. It is, however, complicated.]

S

Shall we go Dutch?

English women will sometimes share the cost in pubs and restaurants. To suggest this, ask, 'Shall we go Dutch?' It is a most useful and economical expression.

Shiatsu

Shiatsu is a traditional massage technique. English people believe that Japanese people are experts at curing people by using their fingers and palms.

If you feel bored in the UK, persuade English people to take off their clothes and then hit them until you feel better. They will feel grateful to you.

'Is it really meant to hurt so much, Kotaro?'

'Yes, Barbara; in Japan we say, ' 'No pain, no gain'.'

Silences

Conversations in English generally stop after a short time leaving silences. There are different types of silence:

EMBARRASSED SILENCE: When nobody has anything to say.

AWKWARD SILENCE: When somebody has said something wrong.

UNEASY SILENCE: When you are afraid nobody will say anything.

PREGNANT SILENCE: When you are frightened that somebody will say something.

POLITE SILENCE: When you say, 'My grandmother lived in Hiroshima.'

IMPOLITE SILENCE: When you say, 'What time are you planning to leave here?'

| COMPULSORY SILENCE: | When you tell native speakers, 'Shut up!' |
| DEATHLIKE SILENCE: | Dinner with English friends. |

Sniffing and snorting

Japanese people sniff and snort in public. By doing this we can cooperate with each other without words to maintain harmony and reassure each other that we are all equally sick but unable to take a day off work without losing holiday pay.

In England the occasional sniff is OK, but if you snort you must emphasize the swallowing of the contents of your nose. Spitting is not allowed in public in the UK.

Sorry, sorry, *domo*, sorry, *domo*

Domo can mean sorry in Japanese. We Japanese are very polite people and, in Japan, we say '*domo*' whenever possible.

English people say 'sorry' sometimes – but not

enough. You will become frustrated in England if you cannot say 'sorry' enough. Do not worry about saying sorry as often as possible – it will drive native speakers crazy.

Example:

'Good morning, Mr Sarai.'
'It's raining, sorry, *domo*, sorry, sorry, *domo*.'
'How are you?'
'Sorry, not good, sorry, I beg your pardon.'
'How are you?'
'Yes, sorry, thank you, and you?'
'Not too bad.'
'Bad sorry, good, *domo*, I'm sorry, I mean I'm bad, sorry. Why not?'

It is sometimes necessary for us Japanese to limit the number of times we say 'sorry'. Do not worry, you need not feel frustrated. Instead of knocking at the door of a native speaker, quickly and repeatedly bang your head against the door, saying, as the same time, 'Sorry, *domo*, sorry, sorry.' Do not stop until the door is opened or your head is bleeding. At parties, you can use the same technique in the toilet later.

Speak of the devil

When you are talking about someone and the person arrives unexpectedly say, 'Speak of the devil'. This is a useful technique for making the visitor paranoid.

[NB: it can be used in situations when you have not been talking about a person.]

Spit it out, man

Do not use this phrase at mealtimes. Native speakers use these words to tell other people to say openly what they seem reluctant to say.

Example:

'Don't just stand there, spit it out, man!'
'Many native speakers are reluctant to speak to us Japanese . . . !'

Standing on tiptoes

To stand on tiptoes is to stand on your toes and lift up as high as you possibly can. As Japanese men are relatively short and British toilet basins are relatively high, it is often necessary to 'stand on tiptoes'.

Stating the obvious

This is a wonderful way of irritating native speakers and avoiding communication. When someone is talking to you, you need not reply, you can simply say: 'You are talking to me.'

If someone tells you a joke and you do not understand, you can simply say:

'You are laughing.'

After, stay silent – no more words are necessary. *Describe but do not communicate.*

Example:

At a party:
'You are looking at me.'
'You are talking to me.'
'You are wondering why I am so strange.'
'You are feeling uncomfortable with me.'
'I am upsetting you.'
'Your face is getting red.'
'You're spilling your drink.'
'Leaving so soon?'
'I am enjoying being alone.'

Strangling

Strangling is a method of murdering someone by squeezing their throat with your hands. It may be enjoyable but it is illegal. Fortunately, it is permissible to press a native speaker's throat by explaining it as a form of traditional Japanese massage.

'That's a bit painful. Mr Sarai, why are you smiling? I can't feel my legs, Mr Sarai. Are you sure this will help my asthma, Mr Sarai? Everything is going black, Mr Sarai. . .'

[see: *Shiatsu*]

Superstitious hairy colonial imperialist barbarians

English people fail to see themselves in this light.

T

Taxi doors

British taxi doors do not open automatically. I do not know why.

Telephoning

Telephoning is not a problem in England – if you have no friends. Sometimes I pretend. (The number of the speaking clock is 123.)

'Could you tell me the time, please?'
10.01
'Thank you.'
'Could you tell me the time, please?'
10.02
'Thank you.'
'Could you tell me the time, please?'
10.03
'Thank you.'

To finish the conversation:

'Thanks, I'll call you later. What time is a good time for you?'

11.26

Tell me about it

English people use this expression when they have absolutely no interest in the topic of conversation and want someone to stop speaking.

Example:

'I have an uncle who visited Japan, Kotaro.'
'Tell me about it.'

That would be telling

This is an essential expression used to avoid personal questions or to pretend you know something you don't.

Example:

'Are you doing anything tonight, Kotaro?'
'That would be telling.'

This creates an air of mystery and completely hides the fact that, as usual, you will be spending the evening in the company of a bottle of whisky, a TV and a pot of Safeway's instant noodles. It can be accompanied by your best slanty-eyed inscrutable look.

By the way, in Japan we use suspenders to hold up our socks. In England, women use suspenders to hold up their stockings. Nevertheless, buying suspenders in England need not be embarrassing.

'I'd like a pair of suspenders, please.'
'Would sir be buying for a lady, or . . .?'
'That would be telling.'

The shop assistant will now think that you are buying a sexy gift for your girlfriend, and treat you very nicely. You need *not* explain that they are a present for your uncle in Osaka who, like many Japanese, has short legs and wears long woolly socks in the cold winter.

That's a bit much

To be critical but polite. English speakers use this expression as a reaction to unconventional behaviour.

'And then he blew his nose on my curtains . . .'
'Oh, I say, that's a bit much.'

You may want to use this expression to avoid relationships in England.

Example:

'I would really like us to be friends, Kotaro.'
'Oh I say, that's a bit much.'

The English brain

Careful examination of the English brain has shown that there are no physical differences between the English brain and the Japanese brain. It is the same colour (greyish), weight and texture. It occupies the same part of the body (the head).

The English brain, however, contains a secret database. You cannot survive in England without the information contained in this database.

UNTIL NOW, JAPANESE PEOPLE HAVE HAD NO ACCESS TO THIS CRUCIAL KNOWLEDGE. BY RISKING MY LIFE AND SANITY IN ENGLAND I, KOTARO SARAI, HAVE DISCOVERED THE TEN KEY COMPONENTS OF DATA THAT CONTROL ENGLISH BELIEFS AND BEHAVIOUR. PREPARE YOURSELF. (TORA! TORA! TORA!)

1. ENGLAND WON WORLD WAR I
2. ENGLAND WON WORLD WAR II

3. ENGLAND WON THE WORLD CUP IN 1966

4. MARKS AND SPENCER'S IS THE RIGHT PLACE TO BUY UNDERWEAR

5. ARSENAL ARE BORING

6. IT ALWAYS RAINS ON BANK HOLIDAYS

7. GERMANS HAVE NO SENSE OF HUMOUR

8. BRITISH RAIL SANDWICHES ARE AWFUL
9. BLACKPOOL LANDLADIES HIDE THE BATHPLUG
10. NO KITCHEN CUPBOARD IS COMPLETE WITHOUT PEELED PLUM TOMATOES (see *Peeled Plum Tomatoes*)

The Japanese problem

If you have stayed in England for more than seven days, newly arrived Japanese visitors will expect you to help them with their problems. To prevent this, it is essential that you are, from the first contact, as unhelpful as possible.

Useful expressions:

'Bugger off, I am not interested in you.' [see: *Bugger*]

'I am a person who is likely to betray you. Please do not trust me or my company.'

'A lot of people think I'm Japanese. Actually I'm Mexican. My name is Kotaro Pancho Sarai.'

If they do not go away, you must listen patiently and sympathetically to them. Then look them in the eye and clearly, softly and calmly reply, 'That's *your* problem.'

The Samaritans

If native speakers are lonely, sad or suicidal, they can telephone an organization called The Samaritans. The English caller receives help, sympathy and understanding on the phone. I tried:

'Good evening, thank you for answering my call, *domo*. I am Kotaro Sarai, I am a small Japanese businessman. All alone, sad am I, I wish to expire my life. *It is all over! Help!* . . . What do you mean, it's OK if you're Japanese? You are not kind.'

There is a thin line between X and Y

This is useful when you do not know the difference between two things.

Example:

There is a thin line between right and wrong.
There is a thin line between love and lust.
There is a thin line between Kelloggs Cornflakes and Sainsbury's Cornflakes.

There is a thin line between mad cow disease and the result of staying in England for over six months.

To suck up to someone

This is not as exciting as it sounds. It means to flatter someone in order to get some benefit.

Toenails

Every month in England, mark the length of your toenails. If they have stopped growing you are dead.

Tongue in cheek

You say something 'tongue in cheek' when you are 'pulling someone's leg'. This must not be confused with 'opening your mouth and putting your foot in it'. It is important to be flexible.

Trade quotas

English business people do not like the Japanese Trade Quota system. You must accept personal blame. Say, 'I *do* apologize; may I borrow your bread knife?' [see: *Hara-kiri*]

Trust me

English people will say this to you – *be suspicious*!

Two-faced

Like the English, we Japanese sometimes hide our true thoughts, character or feelings. If you are English this is called diplomacy.

If, however, we Japanese are 'diplomatic', native speakers call us 'two-faced' (untruthful and untrustworthy). It is reassuring to find that xenophobia is reciprocal . . .

Example:

'Kotaro, you lied, you two-faced runt.'
'Be fair, old boy, I was merely dissimulating.'

U

Underground station platforms

In Japan, trains always arrive on the right and leave on the left. In England this is not true. To escape after pushing native speakers under trains, choose victims near an exit. There is a new system for buying multiple tickets on the London Underground – it is much more convenient.

V

Vending machines

Life is not worth living without vending machines. I miss them. I miss them terribly . . .

Vocabulary

Because the English have many different words for the same thing, they believe many things are different. This is a trap. They are all the same.

Example:

French, Germans, Chinese, Arabs, Indians, Americans and Eskimos are all *foreign*.

W

Waiting for trains

In Japan we salarymen practise imaginary golf strokes to pass the time while waiting for the train. In England, practise imaginary cricket strokes and whistle 'Colonel Bogey' [see *Colonel Bogey's March*].

Whales

Some English people do not like the Japanese, but most love whales. Like cats, dogs and goldfish they are known as friendly and trustworthy creatures – unlike the Japanese. If you are attacked on this issue, try saying:

I, personally, have never killed a whale. In Japan, I was always too busy.

Or

'I am a Catholic. We Japanese Catholics only eat whale on Friday.'

Or

'I agree, I often wonder where Moby Dick is now. Captain Ahab was a bad role model.'

What does your name mean in Japanese?

When native speakers first discover that Japanese names have meanings, they continually ask this stupid, boring question.

Example:

'What does Kotaro mean?'
' "Ko" means wide, big, large, broad (minded). "Taro" is a typical traditional Japanese boy's name. When I was born on 26 October 1970 (it was a really bright and clear day). My parents named me "Kotaro" hoping I would be big, great and broad-minded. Really, I am very tiny, incredibly nasty and extremely narrow-minded – like my father. That's why when I asked my parents what my name meant, they just stared at me awhile and smiled and went out of my room without saying anything. Now that you understand what my name means, what do you think about this sad story? Are you not ashamed that you asked? Are you feeling sorry

for me? Are you feeling sorry for my parents? Have you no feelings at all?'

Alternatively reply, 'If you must know, it means "homicidal Ninja who hates people asking questions".

It is often worth researching some English names: 'Ah, Barbara; that is Greek for someone who talks nonsense . . .'

What is it this time?

Like some missile defence systems, this phrase enables you to strike before you are attacked. Do not hesitate to use this phrase if people look at you and begin to speak.

Example:

'Kotaro, would you mind . . .'
'What is it this time?'

'Kotaro, could . . .'
'What is it this time?'

'Kotaro . . .'
'What is it this time?'

'Kot . . .'
'What is it this time?'

'K . . .'
'What is it this time?'

Instead of saying, 'What time is it?', glance at someone's watch, then stare and say, 'What is it this time?'

The English word for the reaction is 'bemusement'.

What is your favourite breakfast food?

To avoid future contact, answer: 'Raw whale' [see *Whales*].

To maintain contact, answer: 'Boiled eggs with Marmite soldiers' [see: *Boiled eggs and Marmite soldiers*].

What's it got to do with you?

Often you will be asked the same questions again and again and again and again . . . and again.

Example:

Do you have a girlfriend in Japan?
What did you do at the weekend?
Do you like English food?
How are you?
It's a lovely day, isn't it?

If you feel impatient you can prevent further questions by replying, 'What's it got to do with you?' This means that the question is too personal to be answered.

If you continue to do this, very few people will speak to you again.

Where are you from in Japan?

Always answer 'near Tokyo'. Tokyo is usually the only place English people know. Very few English people know where Tokyo is anyway.

While there is life, there is hope

Untrue in England.

Why are we Japanese yellow?

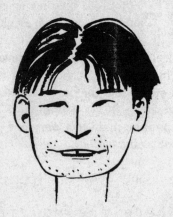

I cannot answer this question.

Why is it always me?

English people say this when they feel that life is not fair. In England you will often feel you are a victim of unfair situations. You are right. That is life.

Willy

English men sometimes call their sexual equipment 'a willy'. We Japanese suspect that English willies are huger than Japanese willies. This is true. I have made a study of the shadows on toilet walls.

You must:

Avoid showers with transparent curtains.
Not buy a kilt.
Stand close to the wall in public toilets.
Not buy tight jeans.
Wear boxer shorts in bed.

Wink

To wink is to close one eye and open it again immediately. It is not a disease. It is a sign of friendship. We, the Japanese, do not wink, but we can blink. To wink, hold one eye open using your fingertips and blink.

World War II

This is a difficult subject to discuss with British people. To avoid arguments you must apologize:

'I apologize for starting World War II, I promise not to do it again.'

Would you mind if . . .?

These words are used to introduce a request of some kind. Generally, English people answer automatically: 'No, I don't mind,' or, 'Not at all.' Generally Japanese people answer politely: 'Yes, I don't.' My response is, 'Yes, I bloody do.'

Wouldn't you like to know

This means I know the answer to your question but I am not going to tell you.

Example:

'What are you thinking, Mr Sarai?'
'Wouldn't you like to know.'

Wrinkles

Wrinkles are small lines which develop on the skin as we get older. The British develop more wrinkles than the Japanese, perhaps because of the climate, the postwar collapse of the British Empire, love of Marmite [see: *Boiled eggs and Marmite sandwiches*] and lack of vending machines [see: *Vending machines*]. Consequently, it is difficult to guess the age of Western people. In general, they are five years younger than they look.

Wrong words

We Japanese often use the wrong words. *Do not worry; native speakers must learn Japanese English.*

Examples:

'How are things in Japan, Kotaro?'
'Japan is in recession, Japanese families are finding it difficult to make ends eat.'

'Look how he's wagging his tail. Fido really seems to like you, Kotaro!'
'I think all dogs should be spaded.'

'Enjoying your egg, Kotaro?'
'It's not cracked up what it's meant to be.'

'Good morning, it's Kotaro Sarai, I'd like to speak to a Dick in your office.'

'Then, we are agreed, Mr Sarai?'
'Your offer is not enough, it is just a spit in the bucket.'

'Do you like our garden, Mr Sarai?'
'People who live in stone houses shouldn't grow grass.'

Finally . . .

'Are Japanese people really so cruel?'
'Certainly not, we should nip that one in the blood.'

Y

You're going to like this

When your hostess serves some typical English dish she will say, 'You're going to like this.' It is not a prediction; it is an order.

You might find

When English people use this expression they really mean 'you will find'.

Examples:

'You might find the roads busy, Kotaro.'
This means you will be sitting in a traffic jam for five hours.

'You might find him uncooperative.'
This means you will receive no help.
'You might find the taste unusual.'
This means you will probably vomit.

You took the words right out of my mouth

When you are trying to reply to a difficult question, English people often complete your answer incorrectly.

When this happens, say: 'You took the words right out of my mouth,' and smile gratefully.

Your English is very good

Do not believe this. They are lying! English people say this when they cannot think of anything else to say. This is called flattery in England.

You're an angel

To Julie, for your patience, understanding and brilliant typing! Love from Colin and Kotaro. Thank you. Sorry, sorry, *domo*, *domo*, excuse me, sorry!

Kotaro's Message to Readers

Dear Reader

Thank you for buying this book. Did you enjoy this book?

Generally speaking, we don't need much time to read books which we are *really* interested in. I suspect that it didn't take you a long time to finish the book.

Am I right?

IF YOU ANSWER 'YES' TO THE ABOVE QUESTION, READ THIS BOOK AGAIN FROM THE BEGINNING. YOU SHOULD HAVE READ IT MUCH MORE CAREFULLY AND SERIOUSLY.

Anyway, without a doubt, I believe you will recommend this book to your friends.

Just one thing, do not lend them your book. Tell them to buy their own book. Remember CIRCULATION IS VERY IMPORTANT.

Thanking you in advance for your cooperation.

Lots of love,
Kotaro

P.S. If you want to tell us your thoughts about this book. Thanks, but no thanks!

P.P.S. I've left my address in Japan for you with my publisher. If any of you come near my house, I'll set the dog on you . . . It's my joke!

Thank you very much and have a happy Christmas.